Careers in Forensics™

Careers in
Criminal Profiling

Fig. A

Janey Levy

rosen publishing's
rosen
central

New York

Published in 2008 by The Rosen Publishing Group, Inc.
29 East 21st Street, New York, NY 10010

Copyright © 2008 by The Rosen Publishing Group, Inc.

First Edition

Library of Congress Cataloging-in-Publication Data

Levy, Janey.
Careers in criminal profiling / Janey Levy.—1st ed.
    p. cm.—(Careers in forensics)
Includes bibliographical references and index.
ISBN-13: 978-1-4042-1342-5 (library binding)
1. Criminal profilers—Vocational guidance. 2. Criminal behavior, Prediction of—Juvenile literature. I. Title.
HV6080.L55 2008
363.25—dc22

                                                                  2007034843

Manufactured in the United States of America

On the cover: A Los Angeles, California, police officer examines a print-out of criminal suspects..

Contents

You've probably heard the word "forensics." It describes the scientific work of crime scene investigators, which helps identify and convict criminals. You may also have heard it applied to the activities of the debate club at your school. So you may wonder what exactly "forensics" means and how it can apply to such different activities.

"Forensic" comes from the Latin word *forensis*, which means "public" or "of the forum." In ancient Rome, the forum was the city's government and legal center, where the law courts were located. It was also a public space where people went to hear famous speakers. So that's how "forensic" came to apply to both crime scene investigation and debating.

"Forensic science" is the proper term for the work of crime scene investigators. It includes fields such as fingerprint and DNA (deoxyribonucleic acid) analysis. It also includes criminal profiling.

Criminal profiling attempts to determine the kind of person who committed a particular crime or series of crimes. It's based on the idea that behavior reflects personality.

A profiler analyzes a crime scene to determine what happened and *how* it happened. This analysis provides the profiler with information about the behavior of the unknown person, or subject (UNSUB), who committed the crime or crimes. From that, the profiler can draw conclusions about the UNSUB's personality. That in turn provides clues about the UNSUB's age, education, social position, appearance, and other factors.

Criminal profiling is less of a "hard" science than other forensic science fields. It depends a great deal on the profiler's experience and is as much an art as a science. By itself, profiling won't solve a crime. It can't conclusively identify the criminal the way DNA or a fingerprint can. However, it can indicate what direction an investigation should take and narrow the list of suspects. This can greatly improve the chances that an UNSUB will be identified and captured.

Forensic science is currently an immensely popular subject in the entertainment industry. The success of the television series *CSI: Crime Scene Investigation* led to the creation of *CSI: Miami* and *CSI: New York*. In addition, books based on the television series have appeared. There's also the television series *NCIS*, which features the navy's criminal investigative service.

Movies and television programs specifically about criminal profiling have also become popular. You may have heard of the book *The Silence of the Lambs*, which was made into a popular movie. In it, FBI (Federal Bureau of Investigation) agents use the help of a convicted serial killer to construct a profile of an UNSUB

In this scene from the popular television series *CSI: New York*, crime scene investigators Stella and Mac examine evidence at a crime scene as they track a serial killer.

who has committed an unsolved series of murders. In the television series *Law & Order: Criminal Intent*, police detectives use profiling to help solve cases. The popular television series *Criminal Minds* features an FBI team of profilers.

These various forms of popular entertainment provide a peek into the world of forensic science and profiling. Since their goal is to entertain, however, we can't depend on them to give us a completely faithful picture. So let's take a closer look at criminal profiling and the job of the profiler.

Catching Criminals with Profiling

Many people think of the FBI's well-known Behavioral Analysis Unit (BAU) when they think of profiling. This unit was established in 1972. However, profiling is much older than that. It goes back at least to the late 1800s. Since then, it has developed into a helpful tool for catching criminals. Among the most famous criminals captured with the help of profiling are the Mad Bomber, the Vampire of Sacramento, and the Genesee River Killer.

The Mad Bomber

In November 1940, a small bomb was found at the New York City electric company Consolidated Edison (Con Edison). The bomb didn't explode, and no one took it very seriously. But then a similar bomb was found on a street ten months later. This bomb didn't explode either, but now police were concerned.

The United States entered World War II shortly after that, in December 1941. Police received a note written in neat capital letters. The writer promised not to make more bombs until the war ended. The promise was kept.

Profiling Jack the Ripper

The earliest known effort to create a criminal profile occurred in 1888. A man who became known as Jack the Ripper committed a horrible series of murders in London, England. His victims were all women. He slit their throats and cut open their bodies. Police were having no luck catching the murderer. They requested help from Dr. Thomas Bond, a police surgeon who examined one of the victims. He studied the wound patterns and tried to reconstruct how the murders happened. Then he constructed a profile of the killer. Dr. Bond said the killer was strong, since he easily overpowered his victims. He was daring, since he killed most of them in public places. Nothing about him frightened his victims, so he was most likely quiet, average looking, middle aged, and neatly dressed. He probably wore a cloak or long coat to cover the blood that got all over him. He was likely to be solitary, with odd habits and no regular job. The murders stopped, but the killer was never caught. Since then, many people have identified men they believe were Jack the Ripper, but the truth will probably never be known.

However, notes continued to be sent to Con Edison, newspapers, stores, and hotels. The war ended in 1945, and still there were no bombs. Police hoped the "Mad Bomber," as they called him, had either ended his campaign or died.

Then, in March 1950, an unexploded bomb was found in a train station. A bomb in a telephone booth soon followed. That bomb exploded. Fortunately, no one was injured. The Mad Bomber sent letters to newspapers saying there would be more bombs. And there were more, all in public places. The bombings continued through 1956. Some explosions injured people. The Mad Bomber sent a letter to a newspaper, promising to continue until Con Edison was brought to justice. In another letter, the bomber explained that he had become permanently disabled while working at the electric company and received no compensation.

New York City police figured many people had been injured at Con Edison over the years. So they didn't think the letter's information was specific enough to make it worth going through the company's records. Desperate, they asked psychiatrist James Brussel for help. Dr. Brussel reviewed the notes and letters as well as everything else in the police file. He studied things such as the way the bomber formed his neat capital letters and the language he used. Then Dr. Brussel constructed a profile of the Mad Bomber. He said the bomber was about fifty years old, single, and living with older relatives. He had been born in eastern Europe. He was paranoid, religious, and well-built; had no beard or mustache; wore double-breasted suits; and lived in Connecticut.

George Metesky *(center)*, the smiling man wearing glasses, is the Mad Bomber. He's shown here being escorted into the Waterbury, Connecticut, police station after his confession.

Another letter arrived at a newspaper. The bomber said he had been injured on September 5, 1931. With that piece of specific information, police decided to search Con Edison's records. They found that George Metesky had been injured that day. The facts about him closely matched Dr. Brussel's profile. He was fifty-two years old and single, and he lived with two elderly sisters. His parents were Polish. He was paranoid, Catholic, and well-built; had no beard or mustache; wore double-breasted suits; and lived in

Connecticut. Police arrested Metesky, and he confessed. Because of his mental illness, he was found not fit to stand trial and was sent to a hospital. This case may have been the first where profiling helped catch a criminal.

The Vampire of Sacramento

On January 23, 1978, David Wallin found his wife, Terry, dead in their home near Sacramento, California. She had been stabbed repeatedly. Her body had been cut open. Evidence also suggested the killer had drunk some of her blood. David ran screaming to a neighbor's house, and the neighbor called the police.

After seeing the horrifying crime scene, police contacted Russ Vorpagel, the local FBI agent. Vorpagel believed the killer would strike again. He contacted profiler Robert Ressler at FBI headquarters in Quantico, Virginia. Ressler was already planning a trip to California. He arranged to visit the Sacramento crime scene. In the meantime, he profiled the UNSUB using information Vorpagel provided.

For his profile, Ressler employed statistics gathered by the FBI about killers who had committed similar crimes. He also applied the BAU's distinction between organized and disorganized criminals. Organized killers stalk their victims; kill in a controlled, methodical way; and avoid leaving evidence. Disorganized killers commit messy killings that seem senseless, leave evidence at the scene, and are often mentally ill.

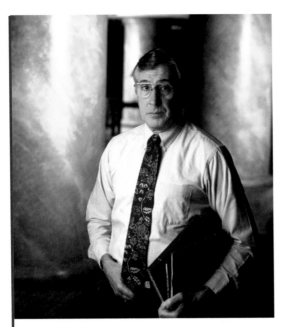

Robert Ressler *(left)* is shown here several years after his retirement from the FBI. Ressler's profile of the Vampire of Sacramento helped police capture the killer, Richard Trenton Chase. At right is the booking photo, or mug shot, of Chase taken after his arrest.

Ressler's profile described the UNSUB as a white male in his mid-twenties who was a loner and probably a paranoid schizophrenic. He was thin and not well fed or well groomed. He lived alone in a messy residence. Evidence of the crime would be found there. If he had a car, it was also messy. He was unemployed and a drug user. Ressler also believed the UNSUB lived near the crime scene.

Police began hunting for witnesses who had seen a man matching the profile and wearing bloody clothing on the day of the murder. Then four more people—a man, a woman, and two children—were murdered in another incident. Like Terry Wallin, the woman was cut open. There was also evidence the killer had drunk blood. The dead man's car had been stolen and abandoned nearby.

Ressler told police the UNSUB probably lived less than one mile (1.6 kilometers) from the abandoned car. That helped narrow the search area. Then a woman who heard news reports contacted police about an old friend she had encountered who matched the profile—Richard Trenton Chase. Police added Chase to their list of suspects. He lived less than a block from the abandoned car, so police decided to question him. They found him carrying a box of bloody rags to his messy truck. He had the dead man's wallet. Dirty, bloody clothing was scattered around his messy apartment. There were bloody objects in the kitchen. Several dishes in the refrigerator held human body parts. A wall calendar suggested he planned to commit forty-four more murders.

The police arrested Chase. He was tried for murder, convicted, and sentenced to death. Chase killed himself in prison.

Police probably would have caught Chase eventually without the profile. But the profile helped them catch him more quickly and possibly prevent dozens of additional murders.

The Genesee River Killer

On March 24, 1988, a group of hunters found a woman's body in a creek in the Genesee River Gorge near Rochester, New York.

Police identified her as Dorothy Blackburn. She had been strangled. But there were few clues at the crime scene, and police had no luck identifying her killer.

Over the next twenty months, at least eleven more women were murdered. Many had been strangled or smothered, and their bodies were dumped in the Genesee River Gorge. Local reporters had invented names for the murderer. They called him the Genesee River Killer or the Rochester Strangler.

All the victims lived at the margins of society. Some were drug users. Some were homeless. These factors made it harder to find witnesses, which in turn made the police's job harder. Most of the victims were found after they had been dead for quite a while. That made it harder to find clues. Finally, the police called the FBI for help.

Special Agent Gregg McCrary of the FBI's BAU went to Rochester, accompanied by Lieutenant Ed Grant, an experienced investigator from the New York State Police. McCrary and Grant visited the crime scenes and reviewed police files from thirteen unsolved murders. They decided that about half the murders followed the same pattern and had been committed by the same person. They prepared a profile based on their study of those cases.

Their profile described the UNSUB as a white male in his late twenties or early thirties. However, McCrary and Grant warned police that this was the UNSUB's emotional age, which might not match his actual age. The profile also said the UNSUB had a history of violent crimes and probably had a police record somewhere. He was ordinary, with nothing especially noticeable about him. He had a low-paying job and drove a basic car. He was probably married. He lived or worked near the area from which most of the women had disappeared. He liked to hunt or fish.

McCrary and Grant also came up with a strategy for Rochester police. The UNSUB had returned to one victim several days after the murder and cut open her body. They thought he would continue to do so with future victims. Next

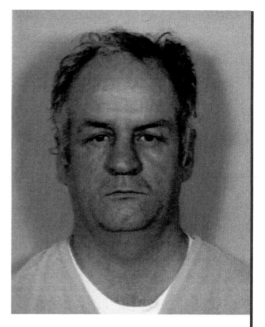

This January 1990 booking photo shows Arthur Shawcross, age forty-four, after his arrest as the Genesee River Killer.

time a body was found, they suggested that police leave it in place and keep watch for a couple of days. When the UNSUB returned, they could catch him.

Then several more women disappeared. Police searched for their bodies in the Genesee River Gorge and found one. And a man was right there with the body!

Police took him in for questioning. They learned his name was Arthur Shawcross and he had spent time in prison for murder. He matched the profile in every way but one—he was about ten years older than the profile suggested. Police had to let him go, since they didn't have enough evidence to arrest him. But they looked into his background. Then they brought him back for more questioning and got him to confess to eleven murders.

Shawcross was tried, convicted, and sentenced to 250 years in prison. He'll never get the chance to kill again.

Chapter 2

The Criminal Profiler's Job

The cases covered in chapter one offer various glimpses into a criminal profiler's job. Now let's take a closer look. What exactly does a criminal profiler do?

The first thing you should know is that criminal profiling isn't a nine-to-five job. A profiler may have to work long hours and interrupt family plans. In addition, there are some common misunderstandings about criminal profiling. Criminal profiling is *not* like other forms of profiling you may have heard about. For example, you may have heard people talk about the general profile of a drug dealer or a terrorist. Those profiles are attempts to create a pattern. That pattern can then be applied to the population as a whole and used to identify the kind of person who is likely to be a drug dealer or a terrorist. However, as retired FBI special agent Gregg McCrary said in a *Court TV* interview with Katherine Ramsland, such profiles don't work well. They're too broad.

Criminal profiling, said McCrary, is the opposite of this. It doesn't create a general pattern that describes a *type* of criminal. It takes a specific crime and crime scene and analyzes them to determine the individual

This FBI agent uses a metal detector to search for evidence at a crime scene. All evidence found will later be analyzed and may help a profiler develop a profile of the criminal.

qualities of the person who committed that particular crime. It's a profile of that criminal only.

Most police departments don't have criminal profilers on staff. This is because most places don't experience the kinds of serious crime on which profilers work. Therefore, it doesn't make financial sense to hire a person who is solely a profiler. Some police departments are fortunate enough to have officers who've received professional training in criminal profiling. However, most police departments facing a situation that requires a criminal profiler must get outside help. In the United States, they often contact the FBI. In Canada, they may contact the Royal Canadian Mounted Police (RCMP).

A criminal profiler usually joins an investigation in response to a request from local police. Occasionally, even foreign police contact an agency such as the FBI to request a profiler's help. The profiler must then catch up on what's happened in the investigation up to that point.

Royal Canadian Mounted Police (RCMP) investigators search property in British Columbia, Canada, in 2002. It was part of a continuing investigation into the disappearance of fifty women from the area in two decades.

Learning the Facts of the Case

The criminal profiler begins by learning everything possible about the crime or crimes. The person who contacted the profiler provides some information with which to start. Police may also send files to the profiler. Other times, the profiler travels to the police department that requested assistance. There, the profiler talks to detectives and other officers who have been part of the investigation. He or she then visits the crime scene or scenes, if there have been several related crimes. Visiting the actual scene gives the profiler a better understanding of the crime. For example, is the crime scene hidden or exposed? Is it a place that only someone familiar with the area would know about? Is it a public place? If there are a series of crimes, how are the crime scenes related geographically? Do they have common features?

Next, the profiler reviews police files and other evidence. He or she may also try to learn as much as possible about the victim or victims. This is known as victimology. Knowing about the type of victims and the victims' activities can provide important clues about the UNSUB. In the process of these studies, the profiler begins developing the profile.

Constructing the Profile

Sometimes police give the profiler several unsolved—and possibly related—crimes. The profiler must determine which belong together and which don't fit. That may be clear with some of the crimes. But with others, it isn't obvious at first. For example, in the case of the Genesee River Killer, McCrary and Grant quickly determined that strangled or smothered women who had been dumped in the Genesee River Gorge were murdered by the same UNSUB. They just as quickly eliminated a woman who had been shot. However, one case was less clear. A woman had been smothered and dumped in the gorge. But the victimology didn't match. She didn't

FBI profiler Gregg McCrary is shown here in 2003, after he retired from the FBI. The profile of the Genesee River Killer that he helped create was instrumental in catching the killer, Arthur Shawcross.

live on society's margins. And, unlike the other cases, the UNSUB had returned later and cut her open.

McCrary and Grant brainstormed. They talked about reasons for and against including the victim. They talked about what the differences between this victim and the others might mean. McCrary and Grant decided the victim *did* belong to the group. Her body indicated the killer was evolving, or changing. He had become comfortable with dead bodies and felt compelled to return and cut her up.

It's Not Like the World of Fiction

Novels, movies, and television give an unrealistic view of criminal profiling. They often make the construction of the profile seem more glamorous than it is; they don't show the hard, slow, and sometimes tedious work that goes into creating a profile. They also often give the idea that profiling always leads to the criminal's capture, frequently in a very short time. Fiction commonly shows the profiler working on the case from beginning to end and gives the profiler much—if not all—of the credit for actually capturing the criminal. None of this is realistic.

Profiling is based on logical analysis and solid criminal investigation experience. Even with a reliable profile, police may not find enough evidence to arrest the criminal. Or it may take months to make an arrest. Profilers are usually working on several cases at a time. Rarely do they work on one case straight through from beginning to end. They offer a profile and some strategies, then leave the local police to complete the investigation and arrest the criminal. The profile alone will never catch a criminal. Even famous profilers have emphasized that profiling is simply a tool. Profiles don't catch criminals. Police do, using standard investigative methods. A profile may help, but it's not enough by itself.

Creating a Profile Step by Step

In any given case, the profiler uses crime scene analysis, police files, brainstorming, and often victimology to construct a profile. So how exactly does that work? Let's examine how Robert Ressler profiled the Vampire of Sacramento.

The murder of Terry Wallin—the only victim Ressler had to work with at first—was particularly savage. Statistics showed that when the victim in such cases was a woman, the killer was usually a man. Statistics also showed that the killer and victim were usually the same race. Terry Wallin was white, so the killer was probably white. The crime scene was in a white residential area, making it even more likely the killer was white. Other statistics showed killers in such cases are usually white males in their twenties or thirties.

From the crime scene's messiness, Ressler concluded the UNSUB was disorganized, with a serious mental illness. He believed the illness was paranoid schizophrenia and the UNSUB had been ill for several years. Since paranoid schizophrenia usually first appears during the teenage years, the UNSUB was likely in his mid-twenties. If he were much older, he would have already committed similar crimes in the area, and none had been reported. Schizophrenics usually don't eat well or keep themselves well groomed. That helped Ressler describe the appearance of the UNSUB, as well as his residence and car. Those qualities also led

Ressler to conclude that no one would want to live with the UNSUB, so he almost certainly lived alone. The UNSUB was too disordered to hold a steady job, so he was probably unemployed.

Advising the Police

Once the profiler has constructed the profile, he or she is ready to present it to the police. The profiler can also use the profile to suggest possible interview strategies. The profiler meets with all officers working on the case or cases, as well as other interested officers. The profiler presents the officers with the completed profile and answers any questions.

In addition, the profiler offers police strategies for pursuing the investigation. For example, in the case of the Vampire of Sacramento, Ressler believed that the UNSUB was too disorganized to have traveled very far to commit his crimes. That meant he must live near the crime scenes. Police didn't need to spend a lot of time questioning people all over the city or considering suspects who lived far away. In the case of the Genesee River Killer, McCrary and Grant thought that the UNSUB would return to his victims' bodies. So they recommended that police leave the next victim they found in place and keep watch. When the UNSUB finally returned, they would catch him. As it worked out, police didn't have to wait. The UNSUB was actually visiting a recent victim when police discovered the body.

The profiler may assist police with other aspects of the investigation as well. He or she may provide information to help police obtain search warrants. The profiler may guide police in the best way to deal with reporters and publicity during the investigation. He or she can also suggest strategies to use when questioning suspects.

Even after an UNSUB has been arrested, the profiler may aid police in other ways. He or she may serve as an expert witness at trial. And the profiler can help police deal with their emotions after the case is over by letting them know what feelings to expect.

Other Things Profilers Do

The tasks described so far are the ones people are most likely to think of when they think of criminal profilers. But profilers do many other things as well. Independent profilers in particular often engage in additional activities in order to earn a living. Independent profilers are those who own or work for private profiling companies rather than for law-enforcement organizations such as the FBI or RCMP.

Criminal profiling has proven useful in negotiating with criminals who have taken hostages. So profilers may be asked to offer strategies to officers who serve as hostage negotiators.

Profilers continually seek to increase their knowledge in order to improve future profiling. One way they do this is to compare the profile used in an investigation to the captured criminal.

In January 2005, Georgia police *(above)* negotiate with a man and woman who claim to have a bomb. Negotiators use many of the same skills required of a criminal profiler.

Another way is by interviewing convicted criminals to learn as much as possible about their thought processes.

Profilers may serve as consultants to lawyers in civil cases as well as in criminal ones. Some profilers also teach. They may teach college courses, or they may teach in special training programs such as the one offered by the FBI. Several profilers have become authors, writing books and articles about their profession and cases on which they have worked. Profilers sometimes even work as consultants for movies and television shows.

Chapter

3

Becoming a Criminal Profiler

If you think criminal profiling might be the career for you, you're likely wondering how you become a criminal profiler. That's a very good question, and there's no simple answer. Profilers need a great deal of knowledge and skill in many areas, and there's no easy, direct way to gain all that knowledge and skill. You'll need a college degree. In fact, you'll need to go to graduate school as well and get at least a master's degree. But there are very few programs that deal specifically with criminal profiling. So how do you get the education you need?

Education

There's no one way to obtain the education you need to become a criminal profiler. However, it's generally recognized that you need sound knowledge of psychology, forensic science, criminology, and criminal justice.

Some people choose to double major in college. For example, they might major in both psychology and forensic science or criminology. A double major is challenging. It

As part of a criminal justice class, students at New Horizons Regional Education Center in Newport News, Virginia, investigate and gather information at a fake crime scene.

demands completing all the courses required for a major in each field in addition to other required courses such as English and history. It's likely to take longer to complete your degree if you have a double major than if you follow a more usual course of study with a single major. Some people therefore choose to major in one field and minor in another. This would allow you to complete your degree in the normal length of time. But you would have less education in the field you minor in. You'll probably receive better preparation for a career as a criminal profiler by choosing one field as a college major, then completing a master's degree in another field. For example, many people choose to major in psychology in college. Then they get a master's degree in forensic science, criminology, or criminal justice. It's also a good idea to take police investigative courses if your school offers them. Profilers need a firm understanding of investigative methods.

Apart from the knowledge gained from specific courses, criminal profilers need to develop certain skills. They need to be able to think logically. Science and philosophy courses can help develop this skill. Profilers need to be able to express themselves well both in writing and speaking. They must write reports and often testify in court. So it is beneficial to take plenty of English courses—or courses in fields such as journalism—that require lots of writing. Courses in drama or communications, which require public speaking, will also help. Studying different cultures can help to understand behaviors and their meanings in those cultures. That, in turn, may help in constructing a profile in a case where the victim or criminal—or perhaps both—comes from another culture. So take classes that help you learn about other cultures, such as anthropology courses. Take advantage of all the opportunities you can to develop the skills you'll need.

A word of warning: If you do research on the Internet to learn more about criminal profiling, you'll probably find people offering to teach you profiling in a short weekend program or through online

Anthropology students work on unidentified skeletons in Buenos Aires, Argentina, at the office of the Argentine Forensic Anthropology Team. The work may help identify victims and determine how they died.

courses. In fact, many well-known profilers regularly offer short training courses. These can be a useful addition to a traditional education or a good way for professionals to sharpen their skills. But while the idea of *learning* to be a profiler through short programs or online courses might sound tempting, they won't really prepare you to be a professional profiler. You can't obtain all the education you need that way. Successful profilers have a much more thorough education than these programs can offer. It's best not to take shortcuts, no matter how tempting they sound.

Start Preparing Now!

You may not be in college yet, but you can still start to develop the skills you'll need to become a criminal profiler. Here are some specific things you can do:

- Take as many science courses as possible.
- Take as many English courses as you can to develop your writing skills.
- Join the drama club or debate team to develop your public speaking skills.
- Learn to take clear, well-organized notes in class.
- Visit your local courthouse to observe trials.
- Participate in volunteer work that will help develop skills or help you learn about the legal system.
- Read books and articles written by criminal profilers.

Experience

In addition to education, you need experience to prepare for a career as a criminal profiler. If you maintain high grades in your college courses, you may have the opportunity to gain experience through internship programs. For example, twice a year, the FBI's

National Center for the Analysis of Violent Crime (NCAVC) selects highly qualified students to take part in a fourteen-week internship program. The BAU is part of the NCAVC. Interns in the program conduct research, observe case consultations involving profiling, and attend classes and training sessions. These experiences provide selected students with an excellent introduction to the real world of criminal profiling. However, it is an opportunity that only a few students will receive. Most will need to acquire experience in more traditional ways.

Many profilers emphasize the need to gain considerable knowledge about case investigation. The most common way to do this is to join the police, FBI, or Canada's RCMP. Expect to spend years getting the experience you need. You'll begin by going through a training program. Then you'll have to work for some time before you advance to the point where you're actually investigating cases. Detectives are the members of police forces who investigate crimes. Someone who has just joined the police force, however, begins as a uniformed officer on patrol duty. You must gain years of experience and pass exams in order to become a detective. More than routine experience as a detective may also be required. Canada's RCMP requires experience investigating major cases, which include crimes such as kidnappings, series of violent crimes, bombings, and arson.

If you're interested in working as an independent criminal profiler, it is sometimes possible to build a successful career

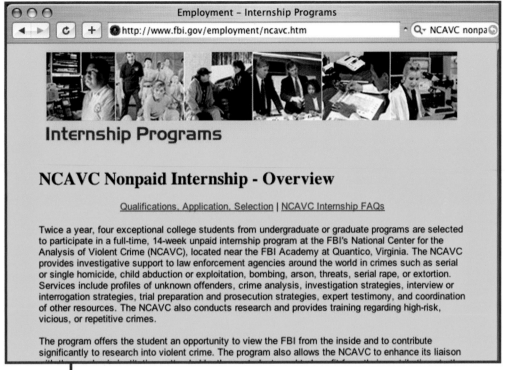

Internship Programs

NCAVC Nonpaid Internship - Overview

Qualifications, Application, Selection | NCAVC Internship FAQs

Twice a year, four exceptional college students from undergraduate or graduate programs are selected to participate in a full-time, 14-week unpaid internship program at the FBI's National Center for the Analysis of Violent Crime (NCAVC), located near the FBI Academy at Quantico, Virginia. The NCAVC provides investigative support to law enforcement agencies around the world in crimes such as serial or single homicide, child abduction or exploitation, bombing, arson, threats, serial rape, or extortion. Services include profiles of unknown offenders, crime analysis, investigation strategies, interview or interrogation strategies, trial preparation and prosecution strategies, expert testimony, and coordination of other resources. The NCAVC also conducts research and provides training regarding high-risk, vicious, or repetitive crimes.

The program offers the student an opportunity to view the FBI from the inside and to contribute significantly to research into violent crime. The program also allows the NCAVC to enhance its liaison

This page from the Federal Bureau of Investigation (FBI) Web site gives information about the National Center for the Analysis of Violent Crime (NCAVC) internship. The BAU is part of the NCAVC, and interns will have the chance to learn about the FBI's profiling methods.

without spending years on a police force or at the FBI or RCMP. For example, Pat Brown, who runs her own criminal-profiling agency in Minneapolis, Minnesota, doesn't have a background in law enforcement. However, she does have a master's degree in criminal justice. And she has done a lot of studying on her own.

Another example is Brent Turvey, a well-known independent profiler from California. Like Pat Brown, he runs his own criminal-profiling agency and does not have a background in law enforcement. He has a bachelor's degree in psychology, however, and a master's degree in forensic science.

Additional Training

In addition to the education and experience already discussed, specialized training in criminal profiling can be extremely useful. The FBI, Canadian Police College, and International Criminal Investigative Analysis Fellowship (ICIAF) all offer training programs for professionals in fields related to law enforcement.

The Behavioral Science Unit (BSU) at the FBI Academy offers a number of courses on different aspects of criminal profiling. The classes cover topics such as how to apply behavioral science to law enforcement operations and how biology, psychology, and society affect criminal behavior. FBI special agents and experienced police officers with master's degrees in fields such as psychology and criminology teach the courses. New FBI agents, U.S. and foreign police officers, and people who belong to organizations related to criminal justice may all take these courses.

The Police Sciences School of the Canadian Police College also offers specialized training in profiling. The course teaches investigators how to think in terms of behavior. It covers topics

Prospective FBI agents listen to information about a "crime" that will take place as part of a training exercise. They are gathered in a mock town that was built for training at the FBI Academy in Quantico, Virginia.

such as the behaviors of criminals and victims, methods for analyzing behavior, and using the Violent Crime Linkage Analysis System (ViCLAS). ViCLAS is a computerized system that allows police to identify and track violent crime series. It contains information on all violent crimes committed across the country and was specially designed to include information about behavior. ViCLAS allows investigators to identify related crimes even if they've occurred in different places. This information helps construct a more accurate profile of the criminal. The course is open to Canadian and foreign police officers who work in a ViCLAS center and have some experience using the system (ViCLAS was developed in Canada but is also used elsewhere).

Graduates of the FBI training program, working with the FBI, created the ICIAF. It provides training in criminal investigative analysis, which includes criminal profiling. The course is open to police officers from around the world. They must pass a challenging program that includes casework analysis and exams.

Once you finally have the education, experience, and training you need, you're ready to look for a job.

Careers for Criminal Profilers

There are few full-time career opportunities for criminal profilers. Most full-time positions are with agencies such as the FBI or the RCMP. The FBI's Behavioral Analysis Unit hires only experienced FBI agents. Out of about 13,000 FBI agents, fewer than fifty are full-time profilers. The RCMP hires only police officers with experience in the investigation of violent crime. Some large police departments now have their own behavioral science units. These probably offer the best chance to find work as a full-time profiler.

Since there are so few full-time positions, they're highly competitive. Many people will be applying for them, but only a few will have all the necessary qualifications, do well in the selection process, and have the luck needed to obtain the job. But don't give up hope. There are other career possibilities for criminal profilers.

Independent Profilers

Independent profilers are those who don't work in law enforcement but instead own or work for a private

James McNamara, an FBI supervisory special agent, is a profiler and an expert on stalking crimes. He has written about his work and provided expert testimony at trials.

company that provides criminal profiling services. Some independent profilers are individuals who have established their own companies after retiring from careers in law enforcement. That means it is possible to continue a career in profiling even after leaving long careers with law enforcement agencies. But we're more interested in independent profilers without this type of background. Let's look more closely at these independent profilers and the services they provide.

What It Takes

Many independent profilers may not have extensive experience in investigation with law enforcement agencies. However, they have at least a master's degree and have focused their studies on fields such as criminal justice, psychology, forensic science, and criminology.

Independent profilers must also be highly driven and willing to work extremely hard. Running one's own business presents challenges that someone working in law enforcement doesn't have to deal with. Many people find it very rewarding, but it's not for everyone. It's difficult and usually requires working very long hours. In addition to the profiling work itself, one has to actively promote one's services and seek clients. That requires a lot of time and energy. There is also the constant worry about whether the business will bring in enough money to pay rent, bills, and any employees. To earn additional money, independent profilers usually provide several services besides traditional criminal profiling.

Services for Legal Cases

Independent profilers may act as consultants to police just as FBI or RCMP profilers do. Sometimes they're asked to help with current cases. More often, however, they're asked to help with cold cases— old cases that have never been solved. With cold cases, profilers don't have an actual crime scene to visit and examine. They must construct their profiles using only police reports and photographs of the victim and crime scene.

Independent profilers also provide consulting services to lawyers in both criminal and civil cases. In a criminal case, a prosecutor may hire an independent profiler whose analysis can help convict the accused person. A defense lawyer may hire a profiler whose analysis can help prove the accused person's innocence. In addition to criminal profiling, a profiler may provide the prosecutor and defense lawyer with several related services. These include crime scene analysis, crime reconstruction, and determining if the crime scene was staged, or rearranged to conceal what actually happened and throw the investigation off course. Lawyers for both sides in civil cases may use a profiler as well. A profiler might also suggest strategies for lawyers to use in questioning witnesses in court. In all kinds of cases, a profiler may be called to testify as an expert witness.

Services for Unsolved Cases

Sometimes, when a murder has not been solved, the victim's family may hire an independent profiler. The family may hope the profiler can shed new light on the case that will lead to an arrest. Or they may simply hope the profiler can give them some idea about how the victim died, why the police haven't been able to solve the crime yet, and what the chances are that police will eventually solve it.

Sometimes a family hires an independent profiler when a family member has died and it's unclear whether it was murder or suicide. Such uncertain deaths are known as equivocal deaths. The family may want to know what happened simply because having an answer would make them feel better. They may also want to know for practical reasons. If police believe it was suicide, they won't be looking for a killer, even if it was really murder. Also, whether or not the family receives payment for life insurance may depend on whether it was murder or suicide.

FBI special agent and profiler Leslie D'Ambrosia *(standing)* meets with other FBI agents and police officers to review old cases in Miami, Florida. This is one of the first steps in creating a profile for unsolved cases.

Other Services and Activities

Independent profilers also offer services and engage in activities that may surprise you. Some provide analysis for television news programs when the programs report on major crimes. Sometimes profilers host television programs on special topics such as the mysterious deaths of famous people in history.

Many independent profilers also write. They commonly write books and articles for both the general public and other

Former FBI profiler Candice DeLong appeared on a television news program in 2002 to provide commentary and analysis regarding sniper shootings in the Washington, D.C., area.

professionals. Most independent profilers teach as well. Many teach classes at colleges and universities. Others teach courses offered by their own companies. Some teach online courses. And some teach special training programs for police.

Independent profilers may also serve as consultants for movies that feature violent crimes. They help make sure the movies' portrayals of the crimes and criminals make sense and fit what is known about such crimes and criminals. Profilers may provide similar services to authors who write mysteries and other types of books.

Independent profilers may also apply their skills to help businesses develop ways to avoid violence in the workplace. Profilers' skills can also help businesses deal with hiring and security issues.

Some independent profilers also offer services to help individuals who are having problems with a stalker. And some even advertise that their skills can help people dealing with personal and family problems.

Hostage Negotiators

Hostage negotiator is a career that uses many of the same skills required of a criminal profiler. The police, FBI, RCMP, and armed forces all employ hostage negotiators. They negotiate with people who have taken hostages, trying to resolve the situation peacefully. They also negotiate with people who have locked themselves in a building and are threatening to commit suicide. Sometimes these people are criminals; sometimes they're not. But in all cases, an understanding of psychology and police methods is necessary to resolve the situation peacefully. The first program to train hostage negotiators was established by FBI agents Howard Teten and Pat Mullany, the same men who began the FBI's criminal profiling program.

Part-time Profilers

Some people choose careers that allow them to profile on a part-time basis. Considering how few full-time profiling jobs there are, this may be the most realistic career path for people interested in the field. But it's important to remember that you'll only be profiling

The two policemen with their backs to the camera are hostage negotiators preparing to approach a church where a gunman is holed up. The May 2007 incident took place in Moscow, Idaho.

occasionally. No matter what other kind of work you choose, however, you'll still need special training in order to do criminal profiling.

People who enjoy law enforcement and investigative work may choose to join the police, FBI, or RCMP. It's possible to be a regular FBI agent, police officer, or member of the RCMP and still occasionally do profiling.

Those who find the scientific side of investigation most interesting may choose a career in forensic science. This gives them the chance to be involved in criminal investigations all the time. And in addition to occasionally being used to construct a profile, profiling skills may be useful in other aspects of their day-to-day work.

People interested in criminology, psychology, or psychiatry may choose careers in these fields. Local police departments often ask such professionals to provide profiles in cases of violent crimes. In fact, some people assume that training in these fields automatically qualifies a person to do profiling. However, although the fields do provide a sound basis for profiling, none of them are sufficient by themselves.

5 The Future of Criminal Profiling

Any discussion of the future of criminal profiling needs to start with a look at where profiling stands today. Although its beginnings reach back more than one hundred years, profiling became a formal, recognized field of investigation much more recently. It's still growing and developing. Criminal profilers don't even all agree on the best method of profiling and best background for profilers.

Three Approaches

Agencies such as the FBI and RCMP emphasize the importance of years of investigating experience. Many people in these agencies believe that without direct experience of crime, criminals, and criminal behavior, it's impossible to do good profiling. Other profilers believe an in-depth understanding of psychology is the most important knowledge for a profiler. In the 1980s, a British psychologist named David Canter developed what he called investigative psychology. It focuses on applying established psychological principles to the

An RCMP forensic investigator retrieves evidence as part of a long-term investigation into the disappearance of fifty women in British Columbia, Canada.

development of a criminal profile. Many profilers today follow this approach.

Both the FBI's approach and investigative psychology depend heavily on statistics in creating a profile. For example, consider a series of related murders. Statistics show that the killer in similar past cases was usually a white male in his twenties or thirties. So a profiler using the FBI's method or investigative psychology would say the UNSUB in this particular case is probably a white male in his twenties or thirties. A more recent approach to profiling, however, does not depend on statistics. In the 1990s, Brent Turvey developed an approach he called behavioral evidence analysis. It treats each crime as a distinctive case and creates a profile based only on the facts of that particular crime or series of crimes.

Many profilers follow one of these three approaches and believe strongly the approach they use is the correct one. In fact, some profilers loudly condemn the other approaches.

Getting It Together

For the field to grow further, profilers need to reach a general agreement on the principles and preparation for profiling. In a *Court TV* interview with Katherine Ramsland, retired FBI agent Gregg McCrary noted that there are currently no set standards for profilers. Anyone can claim to be a profiler. Profilers don't have to pass an exam or obtain a license that says they're qualified to do profiling. In order to give the field professionalism, that needs to change. Already, the first steps have been taken.

Brent Turvey wrote a book that attempts to establish professional standards for criminal profilers and profiling. Since not everyone agrees with behavioral evidence analysis—Turvey's profiling method—not everyone agrees with the ideas in his book. But the book makes people think and talk about these ideas. And that's a start.

For a long time, there was mistrust between profilers in law enforcement and those with a background in psychology. That is also changing. The FBI now works more closely with forensic psychologists. Psychologists are even employed in the FBI's Behavioral Science Unit. And the BSU conducts research with forensic psychologists at colleges and universities. This joint work is helping to create a field where investigative experience and the scientific and statistical strengths of psychology all play important roles. McCrary has written that criminal profiling will be most effective when it has added the strengths of the psychiatrist and forensic scientist.

An Australian psychologist named Richard Kocsis has noted that profilers also need to reach an agreement on one other aspect of the field. Kocsis claims that while everyone is arguing about principles and methods for profiling, no one has really bothered to examine some basic questions about the profile itself. He says agreement is needed on what information a profile should contain and what material is necessary to construct a good profile.

While all this discussion is occurring within the field of profiling, other fields are developing that can make their own important contributions.

New and Developing Methods

Several other investigative methods have been developing over the past twenty years, which, when combined with criminal profiling, can be extremely useful to investigators. These include geographic profiling, textual analysis, psycholinguistics, and computerized systems that identify and link violent crimes.

Geographic profiling determines the likely home and work locations, as well as travel routes, of an UNSUB who has committed a series of crimes. It is meant to be used for violent crimes and works best when used together with criminal profiling. Information

D. Kim Rossmo *(left)* talks with the media about geographic profiling and how it can help criminal investigations such as the one involving the 2002 sniper shootings in the Washington, D.C., area. Rossmo is credited with developing geographic profiling.

about sites connected to the crimes—where the UNSUB first encountered the victim, where the UNSUB attacked the victim, where the victim was killed (if the crimes are murders), where the victim's body was left—is entered into a computer. The computer uses the information to determine the UNSUB's "anchor point," which is usually a home or workplace. At least five crimes or related sites are needed to create a complete profile. Some analysis, however, can be done with less information.

Textual Analysis
Catches the Unabomber

1
2
3
4
5
6
7
8
9
10
11
12
13

From 1978 through 1995, an UNSUB sent bombs to people in different places around the United States. Since the UNSUB seemed to especially dislike university professors, he became known as the Unabomber. The FBI searched for the Unabomber with no luck. There were no bombs between 1987 and 1993, and the FBI began to hope that perhaps the Unabomber was in prison or dead. Then the bombings began again. The FBI created a list of suspects that included 50,000 names! It seemed almost impossible to catch the Unabomber. Then he sent a long article to two major newspapers. A woman who read about the article thought it sounded like her husband's brother. Her husband compared the article to letters he had received from his brother and decided, sadly, that his wife was right. He contacted the FBI. With this information, the FBI found and arrested the Unabomber—a mentally ill man named Ted Kaczynski.

Another new method is textual analysis. It uses a computer to study letters an UNSUB has sent to police, newspapers, and other people or organizations. It examines specific ways of expressing ideas as well as phrases and individual words the UNSUB uses. By comparing writing samples from suspects to the UNSUB's

FBI agents surround Ted Kaczynski, the Unabomber, after his arrest in Montana in April 1996. Textual analysis helped with his case, which remained unsolved for eighteen years.

letters, it can identify the UNSUB. An UNSUB's language can also be analyzed using psycholinguistics. This method looks at features such as sentence construction and language structure. It can help reveal where the UNSUB came from originally and other information such as the UNSUB's race, age, job, and level of education.

The development of computerized systems that collect, compare, and analyze violent crimes has also been an important step forward. These systems use some of the same behavior principles that are employed in criminal profiling and help link related crimes even if they occurred in different locations. Canada's RCMP developed the Violent Crime Linkage Analysis System (ViCLAS). The FBI developed the Violent Criminal Apprehension Program (ViCAP), which it provides free to state and local law enforcement agencies. Unfortunately, not all U.S. law enforcement agencies have decided to use it. The system's usefulness would be greatly improved if all agencies used it.

Criminal profiling has grown considerably since the FBI established its program in 1972. However, there is still much more to learn and many ways the system can be improved. Anyone who decides to become a criminal profiler can look forward to an exciting and challenging career.

analysis An examination of something, or the parts that make it up, and their relationships.

arson The burning of a building or other property with malicious or criminal intent.

civil case A legal case that relates to private rights and remedies rather than crime.

client Someone who pays a company or other people to do something.

compensation Payment to an injured worker.

conclusively Decisively or without a doubt.

criminal justice The field dealing with the nature and causes of crime and how the police, courts, and prison system work.

criminology The scientific study of crime as it results from and affects society, of criminals, and of the prison system.

culture The beliefs, practices, and arts of a group of people.

debate The organized discussion of a topic between two sides that follows certain rules.

DNA Material inside a person's cells that determines the person's distinctive physical features. Except for identical twins, every person's DNA is different.

hostage A person held as a prisoner until some condition is agreed to.

internship A position that allows a qualified person to gain experience in a field under the supervision of a professional.

major The subject in which a college student specializes.

minor A subject studied by a college student that requires fewer courses than a major.

negotiate To talk over and arrange terms for an agreement.

paranoid Having a mental illness that includes unrealistic notions of one's own importance or abilities, or the belief that others are out to get one.

prosecutor The lawyer who represents the government in criminal cases.

psychiatrist A medical doctor who specializes in mental, emotional, and behavioral illnesses.

schizophrenic A person who suffers from a mental illness that includes a loss of contact with reality and such things as hearing voices.

search warrant A legal paper giving police authority to search an area, such as a house or car, for evidence of a crime.

smother To kill someone by preventing him or her from breathing by a means such as covering his or her face with a pillow.

statistics Facts in the form of numbers.

strangle To kill someone by choking.

strategy Plans used or created to achieve a goal.

suicide The act of killing oneself on purpose.

Academy of Behavioral Profiling (ABP)

336 Lincoln Street

P.O. Box 6406

Sitka, AK 99835

(831) 254-5446

Web site: http://www.profiling.org

The ABP is a professional association devoted to applying evidence-based criminal profiling in investigations.

American Psychological Association (APA)

750 First Street NE

Washington, DC 20002-4242

(800) 374-2721 or (202) 336-5500

Web site: http://www.apa.org

The APA is a scientific and professional organization representing psychology in the United States. It contains a number of professional societies, including the American Psychology-Law Society.

Canadian Psychological Association (CPA)

141 Laurier Avenue West, Suite 702

Ottawa, ON K1P 5J3

Canada

(613) 237-2144

Web site: http://www.cpa.ca

The CPA was founded in 1939 and includes a Criminal Justice Section.

Canadian Society of Forensic Science (CSFS)

3332 McCarthy Road

P.O. Box 37040

Ottawa, ON K1V 0W0

Canada

Web site: http://ww2.csfs.ca

The CSFS is a nonprofit organization committed to maintaining profession standards and promoting the study of forensic science.

The International Association of Crime Analysts (IACA)

9218 Metcalf Avenue, #364

Overland Park, KS 66212

(800) 609-3419

Web site: http://www.iaca.net

The IACA was established in 1990 to help crime analysts around the world improve their skills. It also promotes the creation of standards within the profession.

Web Sites

Due to the changing nature of Internet links, Rosen Publishing has developed an online list of Web sites related to the subject of this book. This site is updated regularly. Please use this link to access the list:

http://www.rosenlinks.com/cif/crpr

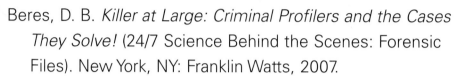

Beres, D. B. *Killer at Large: Criminal Profilers and the Cases They Solve!* (24/7 Science Behind the Scenes: Forensic Files). New York, NY: Franklin Watts, 2007.

Bowers, Vivien. *Crime Scene: How Investigators Use Science to Track Down the Bad Guys.* Toronto, ON: Maple Tree Press, 2006.

Davis, Barbara J. *Criminal Profiling* (Crime Scene Science). Milwaukee, WI: World Almanac Library, 2007.

Esherick, Joan. *Criminal Psychology and Personality Profiling* (Forensics: The Science of Crime-Solving). Broomall, PA: Mason Crest Publishers, 2005.

Fridell, Ron. *Forensic Science* (Cool Science). Minneapolis, MN: Lerner Publications, 2006.

Owen, David. *Police Lab: How Forensic Science Tracks Down and Convicts Criminals.* Toronto, ON: Firefly Books, 2002.

Platt, Richard. *Forensics* (Kingfisher Knowledge). Boston, MA: Kingfisher, 2005.

Stewart, Gail B. *Forensics* (The KidHaven Science Library). Farmington Hills, MI: KidHaven Press, 2006.

Wagner, Heather Lehr. *The Federal Bureau of Investigation* (The U.S. Government: How It Works). New York, NY: Chelsea House, 2007.

Bibliography

American Board of Forensic Psychology. "Forensic Psychology." 2007. Retrieved April 7, 2007 (http://www.abfp.com).

APA Help Center. "Psychology and Law Enforcement—Criminal Profiling." American Psychological Association. 2004. Retrieved April 8, 2007 (http://www.apahelpcenter.org/articles/article.php?id=64).

Behavioral Criminology International. 2003. Retrieved May 24, 2007 (http://www.criminalprofiler.com).

Canadian Police College. "Police Sciences School." 2006. Retrieved May 18, 2007 (http://www.cpc.gc.ca/sciences/scienc_e.htm).

Criminal Profiling Research. "The Case of Arthur Shawcross." Retrieved April 7, 2007 (http://www.criminalprofiling.ch/cases-shawcross.html).

Criminal Profiling Research. "The Profiling Method(s)." Retrieved April 7, 2007 (http://www.criminalprofiling.ch/methodoverview.html).

Criminal Profiling Research. "Various Types of Profiling." Retrieved April 7, 2007 (http://www.criminalprofiling.ch/types.html).

Davis, Michael R. "Criminal Investigative Analysis in the Australian Context." The Australian Psychological Society. 2007. Retrieved May 14, 2007 (http://www.psychology.org.au/publications/inpsych/context).

Federal Bureau of Investigation. "The FBI Academy: Behavioral Science Unit." Retrieved May 18, 2007 (http://www.fbi.gov/hq/td/academy/bsu/bsu.htm).

Federal Bureau of Investigation. "Investigative Programs: Critical Incident Response Group." Retrieved April 8, 2007 (http://www.fbi.gov/hq/isd/cirg/ncavc.htm#bau).

Federal Bureau of Investigation. "National Center for the Analysis of Violent Crime Volunteer Internship Program." Retrieved May 17, 2007 (http://fbijobs.gov/232.asp).

Fintzy, Robert T., M.D. "Review of Criminal Profiling: An Introduction to Behavioral Evidence Analysis, by Brent Turvey." *American Journal of*

Psychiatry. 2000. Retrieved April 8, 2007 (http://ajp.psychiatryonline.org/cgi/content/full/157/9/1532).

Forensic Science Society. "A Career in Forensic Science." Retrieved April 8, 2007 (http://www.forensic-science-society.org.uk/information/careers.html).

Forensic Solutions, LLC. "Case Help." 2006. Retrieved May 24, 2007 (http://www.corpus-delicti.com/casehelp).

Godwin Trial & Forensic Consultancy, Inc. 2007. Retrieved May 24, 2007 (http://www.investigativepsych.com).

Indiana University. "Majors and Careers—Criminal Justice." Retrieved May 17, 2007 (http://www.indiana.edu/~udiv/majors/majorinfo.cgi/57).

Innes, Brian. *Profile of a Criminal Mind.* Pleasantville, NY: Reader's Digest Association, 2003.

McCrary, Gregg O. "Frequently Asked Questions." Behavioral Criminology International. 2003. Retrieved May 24, 2007 (http://www.criminalprofiler.com/faq.htm).

McCrary, Gregg O., with Katherine Ramsland. *The Unknown Darkness: Profiling the Predators Among Us.* New York, NY: Harpertorch, 2003.

Meyer, C. B. "Introduction to Criminal Profiling." Criminal Profiling Research. Retrieved April 7, 2007 (http://www.criminalprofiling.ch/introduction.html).

Nagle, D. Brendan. "Forum, Roman." World Book Multimedia Encyclopedia. Chicago, IL: World Book, Inc., 2002.

Nute, Dale. "Advice About a Career in Forensic Science." Retrieved April 7, 2007 (http://www.criminology.fsu.edu/faculty/nute/FScareers.html).

Pat Brown Criminal Profiling Agency. 2005. Retrieved April 28, 2007 (http://www.patbrownprofiling.com).

Petherick, Wayne. "Criminal Profiling: How It Got Started and How It Is Used." Crime Library. 2006. Retrieved April 7, 2007 (http://www.crimelibrary.com/criminology/criminalprofiling2).

Ramsland, Katherine. "The Genesee River Strangler." Crime Library. 2007. Retrieved April 7, 2007 (http://www.crimelibrary.com/serial/shawcross/index.htm).

Ramsland, Katherine. "The Nuances of Profiling." Crime Library. Retrieved May 14, 2007 (http://www.crimelibrary.com/criminal_mind/profiling/mccrary.3.html).

Ramsland, Katherine. "Richard Trenton Chase." Crime Library. 2007. Retrieved May 9, 2007 (http://www.crimelibrary.com/serial_killers/weird/chase/index_1.html).

Ressler, Robert K. "The Vampire Killer." 1997. Retrieved May 9, 2007 (http://www.robertkressler.com/ex_fights.htm).

Robert K. Ressler Web site. 1997. Retrieved May 24, 2007 (http://www.robertkressler.com).

Royal Canadian Mounted Police. "Criminal Investigative Analysis." 2005. Retrieved May 14, 2007 (http://www.rcmp.ca/techops/crim_prof_e.htm).

Royal Canadian Mounted Police. "Geographic Profiling." 2005. Retrieved May 27, 2007 (http://www.rcmp.ca/techops/geog_prof_e.htm).

Royal Canadian Mounted Police. "Recruiting—Technical Operations." Retrieved May 14, 2007 (http://www.rcmp.ca/techops/recruiting_e.htm).

Royal Canadian Mounted Police. "Violent Crime Linkage Analysis System (ViCLAS)." Retrieved May 18, 2007 (http://www.rcmp-grc.gc.ca/viclas/viclas_e.htm).

Rutgers University. "Criminal Justice Major." 2006. Retrieved May 17, 2007 (http://www.rci.rutgers.edu/~nbcjm).

Turvey, Brent E. "Abbreviated Curriculum Vitae." Forensic Solutions, LLC. Retrieved May 17, 2007 (http://www.corpus-delicti.com/brent/brent_cv.html).

University of Maryland University College. "Criminal Justice." Retrieved May 17, 2007 (http://www.umuc.edu/prog/ugp/majors/ccjs.shtml).

Winerman, Lea. "Criminal Profiling: The Reality Behind the Myth." Monitor on Psychology. 2004. Retrieved April 7, 2007 (http://www.apa.org/monitor/julaug04/criminal.html).

Yount, M. L. "Criminal Profiling." Retrieved April 8, 2007 (http://www.mtholyoke.edu/~mlyount/MySites/ForensicPsychology/CriminalProfiling.html).

About the Author

Janey Levy is an educator, editor, and author, and has written more than seventy books for young people. She is a lifelong fan of mystery novels and is also a fan of the CSI television programs, as well as NCIS and Criminal Minds. She lives in Colden, New York.

Photo Credits

Cover, p. 1 © Robert Nickelsberg/Getty Images; p. 6 © Larry Riley/CBS Photo/Getty Images; p. 8 © Express Newspapers/Getty Images; p. 10 © Bettmann/Corbis; p. 12 (left) © Paul Harris/Getty Images; pp. 15, 21, 26, 28, 44, 47, 50 © AP Images; p. 18 © Luke Frazza/Getty Images; p. 19 © Don MacKinnon/Getty Images; p. 30 © Juan Mabromata/AFP/Getty Images; p. 35 © Anna Clopet/Corbis; p. 38 © Michael Bryant/krtphotos/Newscom; p. 41 © C. W. Griffin/krtphotos/Newscom; p. 42 © Alex Wong/Getty Images; p. 52 © Todd Korol/Getty Images.

Designer: Les Kanturek; **Photo Researcher:** Amy Feinberg